THE SUPERTEAMS

SUNDERLAND

ALL EVERY MACKEMS FAN NEEDS TO KNOW
ABOUT THE 1998/99 SEASON

mustard

First published in 1999 by
Mustard

Mustard is an imprint of
Parragon

Parragon
Queen Street House
4 Queen Street
Bath BA1 1HE, UK
Copyright ©Parragon 1999

British Library Cataloguing-in Publication Data.

A catalogue record for this book is available
from the British Library.

ISBN 1 84164 250 9

Printed in Italy

CONTENTS

Ready For The Challenge

The squad that **Peter Reid** had in 1997-98 was good enough to win promotion – they just fell at the **final hurdle**, losing on **penalties** in the play-off final. Reid decided to rely on that squad with very few additions as he looked to overcome the **heartbreak** and reach the Premiership.

DEFENCE

New keeper **Thomas Sorensen**, bought from Odense in his native Denmark, missed just one match all season. In front of him was another new signing, **Paul Butler**, brought in from Bury. **Michael Gray** was looking to make up for his crucial penalty miss in the play-off. **Andy Melville** was a regular, too. And captain **Kevin Ball** headed the determined bunch. **Chris Makin** figured at the back and further forward.

MIDFIELD

Allan Johnston and **Nicky** **Summerbee** carried the game to the opposition. **Lee Clark** and **Alex Rae** played their parts when not out injured, while **Darren Williams** and **Martin Scott** played in roughly half the matches.

ATTACK

No doubts about the quality of the

first choice forward line – the up-and-coming **Kevin Phillips**, who top scored in Division One in 1997-98, and **Niall Quinn**, the Irish international veteran. They were backed up by former QPR and Sampdoria striker **Daniele Dichio**, and the promising youngster **Michael Bridges**.

IN THE HOT SEAT

Peter Reid became Sunderland manager in **March 1995**. He was boss of **Manchester City** between 1990 and 1993, after an illustrious playing career as a midfielder with **Bolton**, **Everton** and **England**.

Goal-den

After the disappointment at Wembley, it was important to get off to **a good start**. But that didn't seem likely in the opening match against **Queens Park Rangers**, until **Kevin Phillips** was handed a chance from the penalty spot with 17 minutes left. But there was bad news, as **Lee Clark** was carried off injured. The result was enough to spark off an unbeaten month, the highlights being two home hammerings. Only Swindon threatened to disrupt matters, leading for nearly an hour, but Phillips was unstoppable for the equaliser. With hindsight, the **best results** are those against **Ipswich** and **Watford**, who would both have great seasons. **17 goals for and just three against** show what a great start to the season it was, and Peter Reid's men topped the division on goals scored at the end of the month.

tart

Worthy winners!

> **I wanted Sunderland to go up last season and I hope they go up this time."**

Tranmere manager *JOHN ALDRIDGE* tries to explain his side's generosity after the 5-0 win

DID YOU KNOW?

First day victims **QPR** had come back from **2-0** down for a **2-2** draw in April 1998 – which meant **two points** dropped that would have been enough for **automatic promotion**.

STATS

DIVISION ONE

QPR	W	1-0	Phillips (pen)
Swindon Town	D	1-1	Phillips
Tranmere Rovers	W	5-0	Phillips, Dichio (2), Mullin, Butler
Watford	W	4-1	Johnston, Summerbee, Dichio, Melville
Ipswich	W	2-0	Mullin, Phillips

WORTHINGTON CUP

York City (1st Round, 1st Leg)	W	2-0	Dichio (2)
York City (1st Round, 2nd Leg)	W	2-1	Phillips, Smith

It's a battle

Seventh heaven

STATS

DIVISION ONE

Bristol City	D	1-1	Phillips
Wolves	D	1-1	Phillips
Oxford United	W	7-0	Phillips (2), Gray, Dichio (2, one pen), Rae (2)
Portsmouth	D	1-1	Johnston
Norwich City	D	2-2	Quinn, Marshall (o.g.)

WORTHINGTON CUP

Chester City *(2nd Round, 1st Leg)*	W	3-0	Scott, Phillips, Bridges
Chester City *(2nd Round, 2nd Leg)*	W	1-0	Johnston

> **We had an excellent second half, but it could have been better.**

Cheer up *PETER REID!* The gaffer's reaction to a 7-0 win over Oxford

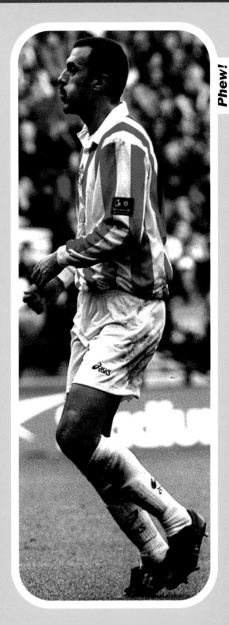

Phew!

Although September was **another unbeaten month**, there was plenty of bad news about. Above all, **Kevin Phillips** went off **injured** against Chester in the Worthington Cup, with a damaged ankle that would keep him out of action for a long time. In the league, the goals weren't spread around enough: just one big win and four draws. **Oxford** were on the receiving end of a **pasting** at the Stadium of Light, but everyone else got a point. Bristol City grabbed an 88th-minute equaliser, though at Wolves Phillips scored in injury time, and at Portsmouth **Allan Johnston** scored seven minutes from time. Overall, it was just enough to keep the team on **top of the division**, but again only by goals scored, this time from Huddersfield.

DID YOU KNOW?

Oxford keeper **Phil Whitehead** came back to the ground later in the season, with West Brom in April, and **let in another three** goals.

Handy Andy

A **third unbeaten month** in a row meant continued progress in the league and another round got through in the Worthington Cup. But there was a **disappointing start** to October, with Bradford – then in the bottom half – coming for a point and getting one. Things seemed to be slipping when Lee Hughes gave **West Brom a 2-0 lead** at the Hawthorns, but **Andy Melville** pulled one back with 25 minutes left, **Michael Bridges** levelled in the 80th, then **Kevin Ball** sealed a **magnificent recovery**, volleying home following a flicked-on corner. Ball was on target again in similar circumstances against Huddersfield, this time with a header, then **Daniele Dichio** saw off Bury with

Crunch!

a late goal. But the dropped points meant second place at the month end. In the **Worthington Cup**, it took an extra time goal from **Niall Quinn** to make progress against **Grimsby**, but the last 16 beckoned.

DID YOU KNOW?

Lee Hughes of West Brom, who scored twice against Sunderland, finished up as the Division's **top league scorer** with 31, but **Kevin Phillips** was third with **23** despite missing four months with injury.

Busy Summerbee

Thwack!

"My players showed real

character

– they never gave up and that is
a tremendous quality to have."

REID after overturning a 2-0
deficit to beat West Brom

STATS

DIVISION ONE

Bradford City	D 0-0	
West Brom	W 3-2	Melville, Bridges, Ball
Huddersfield Town	D 1-1	Ball
Bury	W 1-0	Dichio

WORTHINGTON CUP

Grimsby Town	W 2-1	Bridges, Quinn
(3rd Round)		

A **first defeat** of the season came in November, but all those league draws were banished. Amazingly, **Niall Quinn** scored in **all six** league games! A great win at high-flying **Bolton** was finished by another good win, at struggling **Crewe**, and there were other **away wins** at **Port Vale** and **Sheffield United**. But that last win was a return to form after defeat

Two-nil!

The migh

to **Barnsley**. The Yorkshire side led **2-0** a minute into the second half, but it was back to **2-2** with nearly 20 minutes left. It wasn't another West Brom-style comeback, though – **a penalty gave the visitors victory**. However, the month's performance was enough to give the club a **five-point lead**. In the Worthington Cup, **Lee Clark** returned after three months, helping the side to a **spot kick victory** over Everton, exorcising the ghosts of the play-off final shootout defeat.

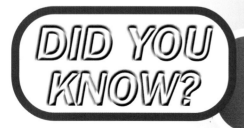

DID YOU KNOW?

Sunderland's **Stadium Of Light** ground shares its name with the home of Portuguese giants **Benfica**.

Blades blunted

STATS

DIVISION ONE

Bolton Wand	W	3-0	Johnston, Quinn, Bridges
Crewe Alex	W	4-1	Dichio, Gray, Quinn, Bridges
Grimsby Town	W	3-1	Smith (2), Quinn
Port Vale	W	2-0	Aspin (o.g.), Quinn
Barnsley	L	2-3	Scott (pen), Quinn
Sheffield United	W	4-0	Quinn (2), Bridges (2)

WORTHINGTON CUP

Everton	D	1-1	Bridges

*(4th Round – **Sunderland win 5-4 on penalties**)*

ty

Quinn

" I feel a little bit sorry for Sheffield United because they caught us on a day when we gave **our best** performance of the season. "

REID after the 4-0 win

An **unhappy Christmas present**, but the rest was pretty good. The month started with a **3-0 win over Luton** in the **Worthington Cup** to take the club to the **semi-finals**. It was closer than it sounds, with **two** goals coming in the **last two minutes**. In the league, it was a case of doing just about enough to start with to maintain and stretch the lead, with **three straight home wins** over unimpressive opponents. But away from the Stadium of Light, Birmingham, in the chasing pack, were good enough for a draw, then **Tranmere** gained **revenge** on Boxing Day for the 5-0 defeat they suffered in August. Crewe were then beaten back at home, though, and the **lead** at the end of the month was up to **eight points**. Another boost was the return of **Alex Rae**, who had had injury problems but had worked hard to get back after two months.

DID YOU KNOW?

So high were the **fans' expectations**, that the team were **booed off** at Christmas when strugglers **Crewe** were only beaten **2-0**!

Taking the Michael

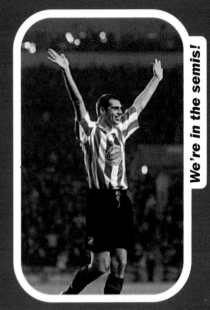

We're in the semis!

> **Alex's response was**
> # top class."

REID on Alex Rae's return to the side

STATS

DIVISION ONE

Stockport C	W	1-0	Summerbee
Port Vale	W	2-0	Smith, Butler
Crystal Palace	W	2-0	Scott (pen), Dichio
Birmingham C	D	0-0	
Tranmere Rovers	L	0-1	
Crewe Alex	W	2-0	Dichio, Bridges

WORTHINGTON CUP

Luton Town (5th Round)	W	3-0	Johnson (o.g.), Bridges, Quinn

Gr-rae-t!

Tough new year

A **hard month**, with more defeats than in the rest of the season so far, but it started well, with FA Cup victory over Lincoln then **Kevin Phillips' return** after nearly four months out. He marked it with a goal at QPR, though the home side recovered to lead 2-1 and it needed a last-minute **header** from **Niall Quinn** to rescue a point after **Kevin Ball** had been **sent off**. Quinn then grabbed two to beat Ipswich, but then things started to go wrong. **Blackburn** knocked the team out of the **FA Cup**, a game

Where's Niall?

which sadly was Alex Rae's last of the season. Then **Leicester** won the first leg of the **Worthington Cup** semi, though Gavin McCann's lofted free kick evaded everyone to pull a goal back. **Watford** then won in the **league**, and the result was the lead being trimmed to seven points.

> **Whatever happens in the second leg,** **WE won't lose** **sight of the league.**
>
> *REID* **states his priorities after the Worthington Cup semi**

JANUARY

Quinn-tum leap

STATS

DIVISION ONE

QPR	D	2-2	Phillips, Quinn
Ipswich Town	W	2-1	Quinn (2)
Watford	L	1-2	Quinn

WORTHINGTON CUP

Leicester City	L	1-2	McCann
(Semi-Final, 1st Leg)			

FA CUP

Lincoln City	W	1-0	McCann
(3rd Round)			
Blackburn Rovers	L	0-1	
(4th Round)			

DID YOU KNOW?

Sunderland may not have gone too far in the **FA Cup** this season, but they have won it on two occasions: in **1937**, when they beat Preston, and in **1973**, when they beat Leeds.

Out-Foxed

A **first unbeaten month since October** – but it wasn't quite enough in one important respect. **Niall Quinn** gave the team the lead at Leicester in the Worthington Cup semi, levelling the tie at 2-2, but **Tony Cottee** scored his third goal of the tie to secure a draw on the night and **a place at Wembley**. Alas! But in the league **three straight wins** and a draw was a good return. The best result was against **Wolves**, and they must have been feeling pretty sick afterwards. Earlier in the season it was a last-minute equaliser from Kevin Phillips; now it was a **last-minute winner** from Niall Quinn, turning the ball home from close range. The **lead** was up to **nine points** at the end of the month.

FEBRUARY

STATS

DIVISION ONE

Swindon Town	W 2-0	Quinn, Phillips
Bristol City	W 1-0	Phillips
Wolves	W 2-1	Johnston, Quinn
Oxford United	D 0-0	

WORTHINGTON CUP

Leicester City	D 1-1	Quinn

*(Semi-Final, 2nd Leg – **Leicester City win 3-2 on aggregate**)*

Love-Lee

"It's all about results but I was very **pleased** with the way we played as well."

REID getting happier after beating Swindon

DID YOU KNOW?

Sunderland's best effort in the **League Cup**, currently the Worthington Cup, came in **1985**, when they lost the **final** 1-0 to Norwich City.

Cup defeat

No arguing!

Five alive

Into the home straight. A magnificent month, with **five straight wins** and just one goal conceded. Portsmouth and Norwich were beaten easily enough, but the **big match** was at **Bradford**. Challenging for promotion, if anyone was going to catch Peter Reid's team it was going to be the Yorkshiremen. And it took 71 minutes to break the deadlock, **Niall Quinn** heading home. Four minutes later, though, the striker was **in goal**, after **Thomas Sorensen** suffered a **head injury**! Quinn kept Bradford out, and the three points were secured. Grimsby held out for 50 minutes, then Bolton pulled it back to 2-1, but nothing could stop the momentum of the team who led the league by **12 points** at the end of the month.

Butler did it

STATS

DIVISION ONE

Portsmouth	W 2-0	Dichio, Phillips
Norwich City	W 1-0	Phillips
Bradford City	W 1-0	Quinn
Grimsby Town	W 2-0	Phillips, Clark
Bolton	W 3-1	Phillips, Johnston (2)

Bally dancer

"We're close
now and we can see the finishing line.

REID after beating Norwich

It's party time

An **unbeaten month**, with first a **promotion party**, then a **championship party**. West Brom were seen off with no need for comebacks, and while Crystal Palace grabbed a point, the win over Huddersfield meant a Tuesday night **win at Bury** would seal a return to the Premiership. The relegation-threatened side tried hard, equalising Kevin Phillips' early penalty, but **Phillips** went on to **score four** to get the win in style. Three days later, he grabbed the third against **Barnsley** in the last minute to gain revenge for the home defeat and spark the **title celebrations**. It really was **Phillips' month** – called up to the England squad by new manager Kevin Keegan, he made his **international debut** in the friendly in Hungary, as did **Michael Gray**.

STATS

DIVISION ONE

West Brom	W	3-0	Phillips (2), Clark
Crystal Palace	D	1-1	Phillips
Huddersfield	W	2-0	Quinn, Johnston
Bury	W	5-2	Phillips (4), Quinn
Barnsley	W	3-1	Summerbee, Clark, Phillips
Sheffield United	D	0-0	

Cap that!

APRIL

Fan-tastic!

"The party finished at **7 o'clock** this morning."

A tired *PETER REID* on television at lunchtime, the day after the Barnsley game

Oak-very-well

DID YOU KNOW?

This is the **second time Peter Reid** has been promoted to the top flight as a **champion**. As a player, his **Bolton** team won the old Division Two in **1978**.

Champion!

Sunderland had **one target** left going into May – the chance to become the **highest points scorers** in Football League history. York and Swindon had won the old Division Four with 101 and 102 points respectively; two wins would give the team **105**. **Kevin Phillips** hit the ball in off the post from 20 yards against **Stockport** to level the old record, but **Birmingham**, heading for the play-offs and no push-overs, **took the lead** on the last day of the season. Then, on the hour, Niall Quinn was fouled, Birmingham stopped, but advantage was played and **Phillips headed home** Nicky Summerbee's cross. Then **Quinn** scored from another Summerbee cross from all of **two yards**, and 20 minutes later a great season had come to a **record-breaking end**.

What a corker!

Lotta bottle

Me, frightened of the Premiership?

No fear

...not a bit.

PETER REID after saying goodbye to **Division One by beating Birmingham**

DID YOU KNOW?

The **trophy presented** to Sunderland as champions is the same one that was used for the top flight before the Premiership was started – **Peter Reid** won it with **Everton** in **1985** and **1987**.

STATS

DIVISION ONE

Stockport	W 1-0	Phillips
Birmingham	W 2-1	Phillips, Quinn

★ Kevin Phillips

Few players rise from non-League football to England international, but Kevin Phillips has done just that, and now he's taken Sunderland into the Premiership. As it happens, his former club (Watford, that is, not Baldock Town) will be there too, but there's no doubt that his current employers are expected to make the bigger impression on the top flight. His goals in his first season at the Stadium of Light all but delivered promotion; this time, despite his autumn injury, he helped pull it off.

YOUNG PLAYER OF THE SEASON

Michael Bridges ★

At just 20, of all the current squad, Michael Bridges has perhaps the brightest future. Most of his appearances have been coming off the bench, scoring some valuable goals. But with Niall Quinn perhaps approaching the end of his career, Michael is set for a starring role.

DIVISION ONE

DATE			Opponents	Home/Away	Result	Score	Attendance	Goalscorers
SAT	AUG	8	Queens Park Rangers	H	W	1-0	40,537	Phillips
SAT	AUG	15	Swindon Town	A	D	1-1	10,207	Phillips
SAT	AUG	22	Tranmere Rovers	H	W	5-0	34,155	Dichio (2), Phillips, Butler, Mullin
TUE	AUG	25	Watford	H	W	4-1	36,587	Summerbee, Johnston, Dichio, Melville
SAT	AUG	29	Ipswich Town	A	W	2-0	15,813	Phillips, Mullin
TUE	SEP	8	Bristol City	H	D	1-1	34,111	Phillips
SAT	SEP	12	Wolverhampton Wanderers	A	D	1-1	26,816	Phillips
SAT	SEP	19	Oxford United	H	W	7-0	34,567	Phillips (2), Dichio (2), Rae (2), Gray
SAT	SEP	26	Portsmouth	A	D	1-1	17,022	Johnston
TUE	SEP	29	Norwich City	A	D	2-2	17,504	Quinn, Marshall (o.g.)
SAT	OCT	3	Bradford City	H	D	0-0	37,828	
SUN	OCT	18	West Bromwich Albion	A	W	3-2	14,746	Ball, Bridges, Melville
WED	OCT	21	Huddersfield Town	A	D	1-1	20,741	Ball
SAT	OCT	25	Bury	H	W	1-0	38,049	Dichio
SUN	NOV	1	Bolton Wanderers	A	W	3-0	21,676	Quinn, Johnston, Bridges
TUE	NOV	3	Crewe Alexandra	A	W	4-1	5,361	Gray, Quinn, Bridges, Dichio
SAT	NOV	7	Grimsby Town	H	W	3-1	40,077	Smith (2), Quinn
SAT	NOV	14	Port Vale	A	W	2-0	8,839	Quinn, Aspin (o.g.)
SAT	NOV	21	Barnsley	H	L	2-3	40,231	Quinn, Scott
SAT	NOV	28	Sheffield United	A	W	4-0	25,229	Quinn (2), Bridges (2)
SAT	DEC	5	Stockport County	H	W	1-0	36,040	Summerbee
SAT	DEC	12	Port Vale	H	W	2-0	37,583	Butler, Smith
TUE	DEC	15	Crystal Palace	H	W	2-0	33,870	Scott, Dichio
SAT	DEC	19	Birmingham City	A	D	0-0	22,095	
SAT	DEC	26	Tranmere Rovers	A	L	0-1	14,248	
MON	DEC	28	Crewe Alexandra	H	W	2-0	41,433	Bridges, Dichio
SAT	JAN	9	Queens Park Rangers	A	D	2-2	17,444	Phillips, Quinn
SUN	JAN	17	Ipswich Town	H	W	2-1	39,835	Quinn (2)
SAT	JAN	30	Watford	A	L	1-2	20,188	Quinn
SAT	FEB	6	Swindon Town	H	W	2-0	41.304	Phillips, Quinn
SAT	FEB	13	Bristol City	A	W	1-0	15,736	Phillips
SAT	FEB	20	Wolverhampton Wanderers	H	W	2-1	41,268	Quinn, Johnston
SAT	FEB	27	Oxford United	A	D	0-0	9,044	
TUE	MAR	2	Portsmouth	H	W	2-0	37,656	Phillips, Dichio
SAT	MAR	6	Norwich City	H	W	1-0	34,004	Phillips
TUE	MAR	9	Bradford City	A	W	1-0	15,124	Quinn
SAT	MAR	13	Grimsby Town	A	W	2-0	9,528	Phillips, Clark
SAT	MAR	20	Bolton Wanderers	H	W	3-1	41,505	Johnston (2), Phillips
SAT	APR	3	West Bromwich Albion	H	W	3-0	41,135	Phillips (2), Clark
MON	APR	5	Crystal Palace	A	D	1-1	22,096	Phillips
SAT	APR	10	Huddersfield Town	H	W	2-0	41,074	Quinn, Johnston
TUE	APR	13	Bury	A	W	5-2	8,669	Phillips (4), Quinn
FRI	APR	16	Barnsley	A	W	3-1	17,390	Phillips, Summerbee, Clark
SAT	APR	24	Sheffield United	H	D	0-0	41,179	
SAT	MAY	1	Stockport County	A	W	1-0	10,548	Phillips
SUN	MAY	9	Birmingham City	H	W	2-1	41,634	Phillips, Quinn

FA CUP

SAT	JAN	2	Lincoln City (3rd Round)	A	W	1-0	10,494	McCann
SAT	JAN	23	Blackburn Rovers (4th Round)	A	L	0-1	30,125	

WORTHINGTON CUP

TUE	AUG	11	York City (1st Round, 1st leg)	A	W	2-0	6,277	Dichio (2)
TUE	AUG	18	York City (1st Round, 2nd leg)	H	W	2-1	22,695	Phillips, Smith
			(Sunderland win 4-1 on aggregate)					
TUE	SEP	15	Chester City (2nd Round, 1st leg)	H	W	3-0	20,618	Phillips, Scott, Bridges
TUE	SEP	22	Chester City (2nd Round, 2nd leg)	A	W	1-0	2,738	Johnston
			(Sunderland win 4-0 on aggregate)					
TUE	OCT	27	Grimsby Town (3rd Round)	H	W	2-1	18,676	Quinn, Bridges
			(after extra time)					
WED	NOV	11	Everton (4th Round)	A	W	(1-1)	28,132	Bridges
			(after extra time, Sunderland won 5-4 on penalties)					
TUE	DEC	1	Luton Town (5th Round)	H	W	3-0	35,742	Quinn, Bridges, Johnson (o,g)
TUE	JAN	26	Leicester City (Semi-Final, 1st leg)	H	L	1-2	38,332	McCann
WED	FEB	17	Leicester City (Semi-Final, 2nd leg)	A	D	1-1	21,231	Quinn
			(Leicester City win 3-2 on aggregate)					

FINAL RECKONING

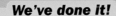
We've done it!

TABLE TOPPERS

League position at the end of each month

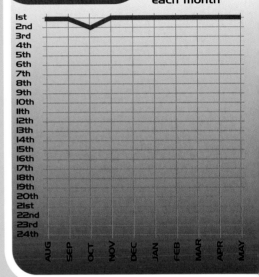

FINAL TABLE

	P	W	D	L	F	A	Pts
Sunderland	**46**	**31**	**12**	**3**	**91**	**28**	**105**
Bradford C	46	26	9	11	82	47	87
Ipswich T	46	26	8	12	69	32	86
Birmingham C	46	23	12	11	66	37	81
Watford	46	21	14	11	65	56	77
Bolton W	46	20	16	10	77	59	76
Wolves	46	19	16	11	64	43	73
Sheffield U	46	18	13	15	71	66	67
Norwich C	46	15	17	14	62	61	62
Huddersfield T	46	15	16	15	62	71	61
Grimsby T	46	17	10	19	40	52	61
Barnsley	46	14	17	15	58	56	59
WBA	46	16	11	19	69	76	59
CrystalPalace	46	14	16	16	58	71	58
Tranmere R	46	12	20	14	63	61	56
Stockport C	46	12	17	17	49	60	53
Swindon T	46	13	11	22	59	81	50
Crewe A	46	12	12	22	54	78	48
QPR	46	12	11	23	52	61	47
Portsmouth	46	11	14	21	57	73	47
Bury	46	10	17	19	35	59	47
PortVale	46	13	8	25	45	75	47
Oxford U	46	10	14	22	48	71	44
Bristol C	46	9	15	22	57	79	42

THAT'S PROGRESS?

	1997/98	1998/99
League position	3rd	1st
FA Cup	Round 4	Round 4
League Cup	Round 3	Semi-Final
Average attendance	33,492	38,724

Best
Game

There are **so many great performances** to choose from, and the title was won by such a distance, it's a hard call. But the **1-0 win** at nearest challengers **Bradford** in March was as good as any.

Best
Signing

Thomas Sorensen had a dream first season. The Dane conceded just **ten goals in 23** home league games, **as many as** Phil Whitehead of West Brom and Oxford did in his **two games** at the Stadium of Light.

Best
Comeback

Turning a **2-0** deficit at **West Brom** into a **3-2 win** in October put down a marker to all the teams in the division as to **just how hard** the team would be to beat.

Best
Moment

Peter Reid's very tired, rather hungover **performance** on **Football Focus** the day after the title was sealed was a great sight. After all the **heartbreak** of 1998, he could **relax** at last.

Worst Game

The **2-1 defeat by Leicester City** in the first leg of the **Worthington Cup Semi-Final** meant that the best chance of reaching Wembley was gone. **A shame**, as there would have been every chance of winning.

Worst Signing

Peter Reid decided that **the squad** he had **could win** promotion with little help, as they came so close in 1998. While a **few signings** were made, it would be **unfair** to single anyone out as a bad one.

Worst Collapse

The team **never lost a lead of more than one goal**, but the one that hurt the most was the **second leg** of the Worthington Cup Semi-Final, when extra time was on until **Leicester** equalised on the night.

Worst Moment

Kevin Phillips' injury against Chester in the Worthington Cup **robbed** the side of a **star player** for months, and came in a game already won.

QUIZ

Consider yourself a real fan? See if you can answer all ten questions on the 1998/99 season (Answers at bottom of page

1 Which **two teams** (other than Sunderland!) **won** at the Stadium of Light?

2 What was the **highest score** Sunderland managed in a single game?

3 **Which player** has been distorted by our artist in the picture to the right?

4 In how many **months** did Sunderland go **unbeaten**?

5 Which **team** did Sunderland beat on **penalties**?

6 What was the **largest number of goals** Kevin Phillips scored in a **single game**?

7 What was the **highest number** of consecutive league matches in which **Niall Quinn** scored?

8 How many **matches were left** when Sunderland clinched the **championship**?

9 Which **two players** made their **England** international debuts?

10 What **record** did Sunderland set by beating **Birmingham**?